INTELLIGENT H

KELLY MARKS

CATCHING HORSES
MADE EASY

J. A. ALLEN · LONDON

INTELLIGENT HORSEMANSHIP

For information on **INTELLIGENT HORSEMANSHIP** and
Kelly Marks courses, demonstrations and merchandise worldwide
see our web site: **www.intelligenthorsemanship.co.uk** or write to
Intelligent Horsemanship, Lethornes, Lambourn, Berkshire RG17 8QS.
Telephone (+44) 01488 71300 or fax (+44) 01488 73783

Also available in this series:

Creating a Bond With Your Horse (ISBN 0 85131 795 2)

Leading and Loading (ISBN 0 85131 796 0)

Handling the Untouched Horse (ISBN 0 85131 841 X)

ACKNOWLEDGEMENTS

Many thanks to my former students, now great friends and associates, for their help and advice, especially Nicole Golding on the literary side and Julia Scholes for her wonderful design for the Intelligent Horsemanship logo. Thanks to Jess Wallace and Jane Young for their excellent photographs and also Ian Vandenberghe for his photographs of Casper in South Africa. I am grateful to Casper's owners, Karen and James Portman and Casper himself, for adding to my education in catching horses. Many thanks to Linda Ruffle, Dido Fisher and Brenda Whelehan for their constant support and thanks to John Beaton who came up with the idea for these books and has guided me throughout. Finally enormous thanks are due to Monty Roberts whose generosity and inspiration in putting me on the path to Intelligent Horsemanship has been immeasurable.

CONTENTS

INTRODUCTION

In my diary of 'Difficult-to-Catch-Horses I Have Known' there are two distinct categories. First of all there is the 'wild' horse, or any horse that is truly fearful of human contact, then there is the horse who is perfectly well handled… it's just that he would prefer to stay out with his friends and 'do his own thing' – rather than come in and do what *you* want!

This book is primarily about the second type of horse and how to get him to want to come in with you and generally be a more willing partner.

UNDERSTAND HIS THINKING

The best way to find the remedy is to try and understand his thinking so that you can work out exactly what it is about being caught that doesn't appeal to him. Here are some possible reasons…

• You only bring him in to work and he does not want to work.

• He sees no benefits in coming to you when he is surrounded by lush green grass.

• He sees no benefits in coming to you whether there is grass in his field or not (probably indicating that he has been unkindly treated in the past and therefore does not connect people with anything pleasant).

• He is very 'bonded' to another horse and doesn't want to leave him.

• His mother was difficult to catch and he's learned it off her or maybe other companions whose judgement he respects.

• He has never been handled at all and that is why he is fearful of the human touch.

For the horse who is only unwilling because he has never been handled I advise you to read my book *Handling the Untouched Horse* in this series before starting on the recommendations in this book. Once you've completed that, then follow the advice here carefully. You won't have to keep consoling yourself with 'well at least he'll never get stolen…' soon your only problems are going to be… what to do with your horse now you've got him!

Of course, it is not necessarily the horse's fault that he's always being left out in the field, denied all the pleasures that the company of humans can give him; there are several types of *people* who are just hopeless at catching horses. The main 'sinners' are those people who haven't learned the right body language to use and approach horses with all the finesse of a great bear. Then there are people whose generally unsympathetic attitude is picked up by the horse before they get through the gate. Finally there is a third group who, while well aware that it may not be all plain sailing catching the horse, never put together a well thought out and considerate plan. When asked why they take hours catching their horse when a few simple alterations could completely remedy the situation, they reply, without hesitation at the absurdity of the statement that 'they haven't got time'.

You will be full to the brim of well thought out plans by the time you have finished this book so that won't be an issue. However you will need to work on perfecting your body language, maybe indefinitely. Once you understand what you have to do, I advise that, as on our Intelligent Horsemanship courses, you get someone to video you. Then study how you are doing (excruciating I know!), study the reaction you are getting from the horse, and list ways that you could possibly improve.

HOW HORSES SEE

Horses see life (and everything else) very differently to how we do. To view the world as a horse views the world we would need to have a horse's brain as well as his eyes but it is important we at least *try* to understand this fundamental difference between horse and human.

The horse has the largest eyes of any land mammal and is a typical prey animal; his eyes are positioned on the side of the head and have a huge peripheral field of vision – 340 degrees of the 360 degrees around him. Without his brilliant visual techniques it is very doubtful whether he would have survived in the wild for all those years.

Our eyes are placed in front of our head as they are in other 'hunters' such as cats, dogs, *etc.* We have excellent depth perception and can judge distances easily. A horse finds this far more difficult. He has binocular vision in the middle where he can look with the perspective of two eyes. He can find it difficult to focus on objects directly in front of him. He has to do it deliberately – and when he does, he cannot see in the other directions.

Remember...

- A horse has two narrow 'blind' spots – one immediately behind him which is blocked by the width of his own body, and the other just in front of his eyes and beneath his nose. He cannot focus much closer than about 4 feet (1.2 metres) so things start going into hazy pictures much closer than that. Do not, therefore, approach from directly behind and if you do have to make sure you warn him of your approach by speaking softly. Some youngsters will back off to start with if you approach them from directly in front, you may notice them lowering or turning their head as they try to get you in focus.

- Because his eyes are placed on the side of his head he has monocular vision to the side, which means he has the ability to see separate things with each eye at the same time.

- He has brilliant long distance vision though he needs to raise his head for this.

- He has an incredible ability to pick out movement so if you are nervous or using jerky movements when you go out to catch him don't underestimate the distance from which he can pick this up.

- The horse does not seem able to pick out fine detail but looks at the silhouette. Don't be surprised if your horse doesn't recognise you at first and reacts with horror if you come out in a new long raincoat or carrying something on your back.

- They have good night vision (at least in comparison to humans).

APPROACHING A HORSE

Whether you are approaching him in a barn or in a large field the same principles apply.

First of all the Don'ts...

Don't look him in the eye! Looking in the eye is a predator action and most horse unfriendly.

Don't walk at him from behind where he can't see you.

Don't walk straight up to him directly.

Don't face him squarely.

Don't rush.

Examples of how *not* to approach a horse

Now the Dos...

Do approach from the front of the side where he can see you easily. He may want to turn both eyes to get a good look at you.

Do keep all your actions very smooth.

Do approach as though you have all the time in the world.

Do walk in arcs around the front of him with your eyes down.

Do appreciate your horse needs to know WIIFM – What's In It For Me?

Do check you can do all the stage one exercises before going any further

Remember if you go into a job with the idea that you've got to do it in five minutes it will probably take you all day and if you go in with the attitude you've got all day it can often just take you five minutes. Please note: this seems to be quite specific to horse handling – in my experience it is not the case with mucking out and office administration.

These photos show the *correct* way to approach a horse

Give a long sigh and have the attitude that you have all the time in the world – that you don't even want to catch this horse anyway. Gradually work yourself closer. Stand quietly next to him for some time before even thinking of reaching out to take hold of him. Although this is how you approach any horse, once he has gone through the Join Up process (see *Creating a Bond with Your Horse* in this series) he will be even *more* drawn to you by these actions.

When you get really proficient at body language and how you can use occasional eye contact, you will know how to make use of a quick glimpse in his eyes just to 'warn' him that you might push him away, you then drop your eyes immediately and move away at a slight curve and he will be drawn to follow you or at least keep his head towards you. This action will bring him to attention very quickly if the other training has been done thoroughly. The best part is that the horse is so much happier with this whole deal because, of course, we are communicating with him in his own language and in a manner that is natural to him.

You'll discover a funny thing… the better you get at using the right body language… the easier your horse will become to catch!

STAGE ONE

Before we can attempt anything more ambitious our horse must be happy to perform the following six simple requirements. Don't expect to be able to catch him easily from the field if you haven't got to this stage yet, so let's first work on these basics.

1. He should be perfectly comfortable with you touching him all over and be friendly and happy with human contact.

Your horse should be completely happy with you touching all over his body. 'You may be already grooming him all over which is wonderful but if he shows discomfort with you in any areas do make sure you are using soft enough brushes and are using them sympathetically. If there are any uncomfortable areas, gradually get

your horse used to your hand moving in these areas by gently massaging an area he is happy with and then gradually extending the area, coming back to the comfort zone and then extending again. Do not make a grab for an area and then stay there come what may – you could make it dangerous for you and the horse. Also don't try and 'trap' him to keep him still. This is another time that accidents can happen – as the horse feels he has to fight for his life. Do this work in a largish area, say 52 feet by 52 feet (16 metres by 16 metres), or your regular round pen. Have him on a long rope or line of about 12 feet (3.6 metres). Hold him loosely, on about 4 to 5 feet (1.2 to 1.5 metres) of slack, but if he moves off sharply, let him 'bump' himself when he meets the end of the rope. Meeting this minor discomfort will help him realise where the boundaries are. Gently ask him back to you and start again. Imagine if you were at the dentist and there were two assistants holding you down. What would you feel like? It would probably make matters a great deal worse. On the other

2. Is he confident and 'cheeky'?

So we will *let the horse tell us* what is the best way to go in the round pen. If he is cheeky and 'having a laugh' and is absolutely confident being handled once he is caught, we might work him quite hard at a sharp trot with even a few circuits of cantering in the round pen in both directions before inviting him in. When the horse comes to us, whether the nervous type or the opposite, we tell him how wonderful he is, give him a lovely rub and put him in the stable for a while, usually with a tasty, small feed waiting.

With these horses my eventual aim is to actually get them 'over- Joined Up'. I will put them in the round pen perhaps as much as three times a day and go through the same procedure. Very soon, maybe in just one day, the horse will choose not to go away from me at all as I release him. He will much prefer to follow me around the pen and this is exactly what I want. When the time comes that I can walk quite fast around the pen, changing direction, and he is still choosing to stay with me, then I can consider turning him out alone in a small, less than an acre (.4ha), rather bare, field. It would preferably have a catching area as well in case of emergencies.

3. Remember... It is a horse's natural inclination to live in co-operation rather than conflict.

Let him sniff the back of your hand first. When you get close enough spend plenty of time petting him. Find his favourite spots. Scratching at the bottom of his mane just as another horse would do is looked upon favourably. Give him a stroke down his shoulder. Don't be tempted to grab his head! Depending on how difficult he has been you may want to leave it at just a stroke the first couple of times. Now go away and leave him alone. Keep working on perfecting your approach before even *thinking* about bringing out a halter. Gradually work your way up to his face and spend plenty of time stroking him on different occasions. Sometimes you could catch him, bring him in for a feed and then turn him out again. When you get hold of him give him a lovely rub for a minute or so then just go away and leave him alone.

A note about catching little ponies

We talk about using body language and eye contact for communication with horses, but this is somewhat limited if we are way above the pony and the only area level to their eyes is the top of our legs. You sometimes hear of ponies that children can catch but not adults. Most horses and ponies dislike anything they don't know towering above their heads. The simple solution here is that for some ponies you need to crouch right down when approaching them or using submissive body positioning.

If you are carrying a headcollar you can keep that over your shoulder for a while or keep a rope in your pocket to bring out later.

> Make sure you never, *ever*, have the rope around your neck – tragic accidents have happened this way.

By now your horse really shouldn't be concerned about seeing the headcollar as you should have practised putting it on in the stables so many times that it should all just be second nature.

BASIC HORSE PSYCHOLOGY

Whichever method you decide to use (and it's surely intelligent to have as many options as possible), do be sure you are working *with* the psychology and nature of the horse and not just looking at things from a 'human' view-

point. For instance, 'He's doing this deliberately because he *knows* I can't be late for work today' is the type of attitude that is of no use whatsoever!

If a mare is good to catch it will make a tremendous difference to her foal's attitude in later life. In the same way your horse's everyday companions will affect his attitude. It is possible that you could turn him back out in his familiar field with his usual companions, and he will not be any keener to come to you than he was before.

When you first go to turn him out with other horses, make it just one horse and make sure that horse is really good to catch. If the worst comes to the worst at least you can catch Mr Amenable and this should persuade your horse to want to come in. If he's going to be turned out with a bunch of wild hooligans it's not going to help your case at all.

Now that you are certain that he is happy with the preliminary stages of training as outlined we shall endeavour to find a way that our horse sees us and consciously thinks 'Great! It's my favourite human coming to take me out!' and even subconsciously that he can't help but be 'drawn' toward us.

Food Glorious Food

A way to make friends with a wary horse is to sit next to a bucket of food in a small paddock and let the horse make his own decision as to when to come up to the food and get close to you. You can eventually move on to gentle stroking of the horse and getting to know him. You should ignore the horse completely so there is less pressure on him and you might even read a book, possibly this one. Mind you, if the horse is very wary you might have time to read *War and Peace* or the *Complete Works of Shakespeare*!

The 'not over-feeding method' has been one of the secrets of the whisperers who can 'cure' a horse or pony of catching problems and soon have them running up to see them. However, if all the components of the problem haven't been looked at, it would not only be very unfair to deprive a horse of food, but there would be a problem again as soon as he got back to normal supplies.

The trouble with using food to catch horses is that if they are in a group there is the danger of taking a bucket out and having them all crowding around you to get at the food. They can often start fighting with each other and a person could easily get hurt in the fall out.

> Do remember feeding by hand can encourage biting and disrespectful behaviour so only use it with thoughtfulness and never let your horse get the idea that he only has to nudge you to get food.

Some horses get very clever about snatching the food and then prancing off at just the second you are about to take hold of them. Desmond, a

cute little pony I dealt with for television's *Barking Mad*, was in the habit of doing just this with his owners. Horses can even get wise to this though and using food as a 'bribe' doesn't always solve the real issues although it is certainly acceptable on the odd occasion for expediency. Part of our work with Desmond was to make sure he knew what 'the deal' was and this was that if he wanted food and to go to the stables with his best friend he had to have his headcollar on first. Desmond was a bright pony and soon got in the habit of doing this. Food is undoubtedly a pleasant association for the horse and so if he gets to know there is always a small feed waiting when he gets in, it's a good inducement.

Make a point of finding out what your horse's absolutely favourite food is – carrots? apples? one of the pasture mixes containing molasses? After all, there are many of us who might not do something for beef burgers whereas we might be swayed for chocolates and champagne…

I suggest that when you go to catch your horse for riding you always bring him in for a small feed first. If you get him to come in for a feed every day whether you are riding him or not that would be ideal. The horses at a nearby farm live in big herds and are called in to the barns for their feeds and a checkover every now and then. It is most impressive when the farm manager makes a noise something like Tarzan's jungle cry and forty black horses all come galloping towards the barns!

If you would like your horse to run towards you as in the *Black Beauty* series just get him used to the idea that calling him (every horse should know his name) always means food or something pleasant. You could initially help the process by taking his best friend (pair bond) out with you when you go to call him. To keep this process going what you must never, ever do is call him in for something unpleasant i.e. injections, farrier, hard work or he'll start to get sceptical. On those occasions, he either has to be brought in earlier for his feed or at the very least you don't call him, just take the time to walk out and fetch him.

FIENDISHLY CUNNING PLANS FOR EMERGENCY SITUATIONS

Trick or treat

For the horse that can be caught with a treat but tends to snatch it then run off, one method is to have a piece of string hanging about 6 inches (15 cm) from the back of his (breakable) head-collar. You approach the horse holding both your hands together, the empty hand slightly in front of the hand holding the tasty treat. As he takes the treat you should be able to get hold of the string. Most horses once they know they are 'caught' quickly acquiesce – 'the game's up' they shrug. If this is not the case and he's likely to pull away, much more leading training work is needed (see *Leading and Loading* in this series).

Just pulling his leg

I've heard that for some older horses it works if instead of going to their head you bend down to look at their leg. This can catch a horse totally by surprise as you bend down and ask him to pick his leg up and hold up the leg on the nearside with your right hand whilst taking his headcollar or slipping a rope over his neck with your left hand. A horse must feel a bit of a fool when he's been caught this way.

Are you going backwards?

Well you could try walking around or approaching the horse backwards. Again, this 'odd' behaviour can sometimes take a horse by surprise enough for you to get the job done. It's curious to watch when this does work. The horse just watches in amazement. What does he think the person is doing?

For when you're at the end of your tether...

Yes, tethering is an option if things have really got that bad. Certainly people going on long excursions with their horse will tether the horses at the camp side and it's a very practical method in those circumstances. It is not something I would personally feel happy about nowadays unless I had the horse in my sights at all times.

Don't just go out to your horse to bring him into work

You know those people who only ring you when they want something? You know how your heart sinks when you hear their voice at the other end of the phone? That's how your horse feels if you only go out to see him if it's only ever for something for you. You need to take some time in going out to catch your horse just to give him a stroke and then let him go away again (and make sure you ring your friends with good news for them occasionally, as well).

Ever decreasing circles

Well not exactly, but going out and just walking circles around him, whilst showing a complete disinterest in him, can help 'desensitise' a horse to your presence. You don't even have to aim to get that close on the first occasion. Just make easy steps for yourself. Gradually work the circles in closer so you can eventually go in and pet him and started this 'switched off' behaviour from long periods of lungeing in side reins. To understand why he was like this at home though it is necessary to understand how 'Schedules of Reinforcement' affect all of our behaviours, both horses and humans…

'SCHEDULES OF REINFORCEMENT'

'Schedules of reinforcement' are how often you use positive reinforcements or reward. The options are **continuous**, **fixed** and **variable**. In the early stages of working with a horse or, for instance, potty training your child, you are going to reward **continuously**, take every opportunity to demonstrate your pleasure and show they've done the right thing. This doesn't continue indefinitely, (in the case of the child, for instance, once they've started university it would be impractical). After a while, once you are sure the horse clearly understands your requests, you can space the rewards out a little more, so, for instance, he jumps three or four jumps at a time before you tell him he's a great champion and he's sure to win at *The Horse of the Year Show*.

Fixed rewards may be used with horses later in their careers, say, after every showjumping round or at the end of a race. Fixed rewards are very common for people. Some people receive their reward of money at the end of every working day, at the end of the week or the end of the month.

Interestingly though it is the **variable reinforcements** which can eventually become the most powerful. This has been proven in experiments with animals and is easy to see with humans, for instance, gambling. It explains how people get addicted to gambling. There are slot machines around where you can put money in, and chocolate or other goodies are virtually guaranteed to come out. But thousands of people sit in Las Vegas preferring to put money in a machine where they are never quite sure if there will be any returns at all but they keep thinking the next pull is going to be 'the big one', the one that's going to pay off… the point here is that people will go for longer and longer periods of time without a pay off if they've been 'trained' in this way.

Sometimes we inadvertently train our animals in this way as well. Let's think about the cat that miaows for his food. You refuse to feed him, absolutely refuse, it's not his feeding time and you are not going to feed him. After a while, you can't stand the noise any longer, so you give him a feed. What have you taught the cat? The value of persistence. He knows now if he just keeps going on long enough, he gets the reward.

Casper's reward, like any horse that hasn't learned the value of human touch, was to be left alone. Sometimes someone would come and try and catch him for a few minutes, sometimes for over an hour. He had learned to get into a negative pattern of avoidance as he knew if he could just keep his evasive tactics long enough the people would leave him alone for a while. To break the pattern Casper needed to go right back to the early stages of being caught in the box really easily as outlined before and then going back to the corner of the field and having the rope unclipped and clipped on until a new pattern could be established.

Seeing how continually failing to catch a horse could start to 'train' the horse to be more and more tricky to catch and confident about his efforts to get away, you can see how the following method used by some people of 'walking the horse' down could backfire if not followed through. It is not a method for anyone who lacks resolve and needs to be thought through very carefully.

'WALKING HIM DOWN'

In Clive Richardson's fascinating book *The Horse Breakers* (published by J A Allen), he talks about 'Walking down wild horses'. To quote from that book:

> G.C. Robinson, writing in the *Dallas Morning Star* in September 1928, described the system of 'walking mustangs down'. The skilful Indians also used this method but they even did it on foot. It was said that some 'walkers' kept the horses from water and prevented them sleeping or resting. Working in relays, it took eight to ten days to walk the mustangs down until they could be lassoed. Sometimes the animals were allowed to drink when very thirsty, as when full of water they could be caught more easily.

I have had people tell me that they have approached their horse's 'reluctance' with the same principles when he is in the field as one might when he is in the round pen and effectively done a modern day equivalent of walking their horse down to achieve 'Join Up in the field'. You can get Join Up in the field if you speak 'Equus' clearly. A domesticated horse is going to be very much easier than a wild mustang to use this method on, but be under no misapprehension that one's work will be cut out depending on the size of your field. This is *not* something you take on if you've got to leave for work in half an hour. One needs to be fit as well as tenacious. When the horse chooses to go away you advance on the horse, effectively pushing him away more. This is virtually the opposite of what was advised, in 'ever decreasing circles' where you come away *before* the horse moves away. In this case you keep following, keeping the mild pressure on, but the instant the horse stops and perhaps takes a look back at you, which one would expect him to do eventually, you put your body on a 45 degree angle and walk away a few strides. He'll soon work out 'Hey, so when I stop she walks away'. After a pause of thirty seconds or more as he studies you, gently walk back towards him with your shoulders on a 45 degree angle. Never walk directly at him, it should always be at angles or semicircles. Keep your eyes down. You've got to keep your signals very clear. If he decides to go away you start going after him again.

I have heard of people spending a whole day working like this but feeling it well worthwhile because the result has been so satisfying with the horse never taking the decision not to be caught again! If you can't 'stay the course' though and give up, as we discussed before it can heighten the horse's resolve not to be caught in the future. You will make life far easier for yourself if you get your horse strongly Joined Up in a small area to start with. The horse will appreciate very quickly the consequences of moving away and rather than taking an afternoon or a whole day you could achieve the same results in minutes.

AND FINALLY...

I have a few horses sent to me every summer that are 'impossible to catch', of the five that came this year, three were genuinely nervous and had to be worked with in the stable, putting

the headcollar on and touching *etc* and they took a couple of weeks to get perfect. The other two simply needed the round pen work which only took two to three days. *Most importantly* with all of them – *we had to teach their owners to use the correct body language as well.*

Once a delighted owner came round to see her 'uncatchable' pony and once she had gone in and caught him and then her two children had caught him, they all stood there in amazement saying 'This can't be our pony!' Now, first of all let me promise you it *was* their pony and I am telling you this story so you can appreciate the results that are possible. However, no book is

going to do it for you. No lecture is going to do it for you. *You* are the person who is going to actually make it happen by working intelligently, sensitively and reading the situation: 'Are we making improvements?' 'Is this making it better or worse?' 'What could we do to make it easier still?' 'Do we need to concentrate on the beginning steps again?'

Work with these methods consistently and intelligently and I promise, **you can do it!** Soon you will not only have a horse that positively wants to be 'caught'… he will come and catch you!

Photo credits

The author wishes to thank Jess Wallace and Jane Young
of Moonart for supplying photographs. The photographs of Casper
on pages 19 and 20 are by Ian Vandenberghe.

British Library Cataloguing-in-Publication Data.
A catalogue record for this book is available from the British Library

ISBN 978-0-85131-840-0

First published in Great Britain 2001
Reprinted 2003
Reprinted 2005
Reprinted 2012

J.A. Allen
Clerkenwell House
Clerkenwell Green
London EC1R 0HT

J.A. Allen is an imprint of Robert Hale Limited

www.allenbooks.co.uk

Design and typesetting by Paul Saunders
Series editor John Beaton
Printed in Malta by Melita Press